From Muskets to Rifles...

Fast Play Wargame for

19th Century Conflicts

by

Alexander Hay

BOZBAT GAMES

From Muskets to Rifles...© – 14 May 2023, Alexander John Hay.

For additional information and updates visit: http://www.bozbat.com/

Table of Contents

I. Introduction

From Muskets to Rifles... is based upon *C'est la Guerre: Fast Play Wargame for the Age of Muskets.* This system was designed to provide a fast yet satisfying game play, not necessarily a "realistic" simulation of battle recreation. Bases or 'Units' in the game do not represent a certain number of men or artillery pieces but are abstract representations of force.

From Muskets to Rifles... uses

- a simple command structure to manage battlefield movement without dealing with morale or having the players issue orders,

- a troop grading system so that better trained more effective troops can have an advantage over poorly trained less effective troops, and

- a method to account for casualties and losses without an overly complicated accounting system.

From Muskets to Rifles... is an abstraction. A Unit in the game does not necessarily equal a particular organizational unit, formation in the field, or a specific number of soldiers. Each base is a representation of force, and as such issues such as the size of one battalion, regiment, brigade, or squadron should be set aside. The player should concern himself with tactics such as troop placement, command access, gun placement and terrain features. The goal is to recreate the "feel" of the period, not necessarily every detail of it.

II. Warfare in the 19th Century

How to define the 19th Century? Some would say, "Keep It Simple: The 19th Century began on January 1, 1800 and ended at midnight December 31, 1899."

I believe a more accurate approach for these rules, although an arguably vague approach, would be to look at the nature of armed conflicts during the period in Europe and North America where the changes were most profound, and also throughout the world.

At the beginning of the 19th Century European armies were mostly armed with smooth bore muzzle loading muskets and bronze smooth bore muzzle loading artillery. These armies fought in dense formations of infantry, and they relied upon the gallant cavalry charging in mass to break enemy lines. Not so very different from the weapons and methods used two hundred years before.

Outside of Europe we see a variety of anachronistic weapons and methods, some more recognizable from the medieval or even the ancient periods; armored cavalry, shield and spear wielding infantry, bows, the rare use of outdated heavy artillery, etc.

By the end of the 19th Century we see the introduction of machine guns, breach loading and bolt action repeating rifles, metal cartridge ammunition, accurate and powerful rifled artillery, and even the occasional airplane flying through the skies. We also see the mass production and industrialization of warfare that made these new technologies cheap, uniform, and abundant.

This period of dynamic change, between the age of the musket and the 'modern' mobile warfare we see today, began at some point after the end of the Napoleonic Wars and came to its culmination during World War I. *So that will be how we define the time period of '19th Century Warfare' – 1820s to 1910s.*

During this period we also witness the rise of radical social and political changes which begin the decline and eventual collapse of the Old Order: We see the rise of nationalism and socialism that together brought about the unification of Germany and Italy and contributed to the collapse of the ancient dynasties of the Romanovs of Russia, the Hapsburgs of Austria, the Hohenzollerns of Prussia, and the House of Osman in the Ottoman Empire. We also see the seeds planted for the decline of colonialism and the collapse of European colonial empires. Then there is the rise of new industrial powers in the Americas and in Asia in the form of the expanding United States of America and the Empire of Japan.

III. Equipment and Scales

Scale

From Muskets to Rifles... uses bases which will
represent various Units. Each Unit will roughly cover a
front 500 meters wide with a depth of 300 meters
although in reality the front and depth will represent a
Unit's area of control not its actual area in space. It will
include the area in front of the Unit, and the area to the
rear of the Unit. The measurement of each Unit will
vary depending upon the size of the figures and the
desires of the players. This will be explained in more
detail in 'IV. Basing'.

Army Size and Troop Representation

From Muskets to Rifles... employs an army point
system to help players compare troop types, army
composition, and scenario development. An army can

consist of 50 or more points of troops depending upon the scenario. The Army Point System is described later.

In *From Muskets to Rifles...* troops will be organized into Units. Each Unit will be represented by a single base that may or may not contain appropriate miniatures. A Unit does not necessarily represent a fixed number of soldiers. A Unit of Regular Infantry may represent the equivalent of an American Civil War brigade or some other similar sized Unit. Since brigades, battalions and other Units varied in size each Unit must be viewed with a certain degree of abstraction.

Playing Area and Ground Scale

The optimum playing area will depend upon the size of the bases. If you are using bases of 5 cm in width the playing area should be 1 to 1.25 meters wide by 1 meter deep. This will reflect an area roughly 10 to 12.5 kilometers wide and 10 kilometers deep. These are only suggestions. Many players may find it advantageous to use a different sized gaming areas or different scales.

Dice and miscellaneous items

- You will need at least a pair of 6, 8, or 10 sided dice (or d6, d8, or d10 respectively).

- Markers will be needed to indicate when a Unit is in Disorder. Almost any marker is appropriate for this (i.e., coins, tokens, etc.).

- Other markers will be required to keep track of casualties or losses. Small rubber bands or some kind of stackable marker should work well since each Unit may incur any number of "casualties" without being destroyed. Like the Units, casualties do not represent a fixed number of soldiers killed, wounded, or missing, but represents a loss of Unit effectiveness.

IV. Troop Definitions

Standard Troop Types

<u>Regular Infantry</u> represents the standard infantry armed with a musket or rifle, and can be classed as Inferior, Average and Elite. Included within a Unit of Regular Infantry will be whatever skirmishers that a Unit may possess. These may simply be troops in 'open order' assigned the task of scouting or screening, or a specific type of soldier trained to fight as light infantry. Infantry can shoot.

<u>Command Unit</u> represents either the General or another sub-commander in the army. The Command Unit facilitates movement and combat. Treated as Mounted, and cannot shoot.

<u>Cavalry</u> represents those mounted units that are specially trained to fight on horse-back, and can be classed as Average or Elite. Although Cavalry may be armed with firearms they will be used at such close range as to be considered part of a Melee. Therefore they cannot shoot unless they are specifically allowed to dismount and be treated as Regular Infantry.

<u>Light Cavalry</u> represents Cavalry which fight in open order. Always Average, and like Cavalry they cannot shoot.

<u>Mounted Infantry</u> represents a growing trend during the period. Many units that were called cavalry lacked the necessary training and skill to effectively perform cavalry charges. Thus they tended to only use their

horses for mobility purposes and then dismounted for combat.

Artillery represents the majority of field artillery available to most armies. A "unit" of artillery in this game is an abstract representation of "firepower" more than a particular military formation or number or type of guns. Treated as Infantry, and obviously can shoot.

Heavy Artillery represents the larger field artillery that were rare on the battlefield but very effective. Can shoot.

Horse Artillery represents the "fast" artillery that is drawn by horses. They can shoot.

Specialty Troop Types

Snipers focus on killing enemy combat commanders and generally harassing enemy Units. Although the appearance of Snipers and Sharpshooters began to be more common and accepted in many of the armies of the period, there should not be too many of these Units in any army.

Combat Engineers have the ability to build roads through rough terrain, and build field fortifications. They cannot shoot.

Light Infantry are specially trained to have the ability to move and fight in bad going.

V. Basing

All figures must be combined into Units with figures permanently mounted on a base of card or similar material. The size of each Unit's base and the number of figures blocks mounted on it should be:

Figure scale is:	15mm	25mm	No. of figures
Frontage for Units:	5cm	8cm	
Depth of Unit:			
Regular Infantry	2cm	3cm	4
Command Unit	3cm	4cm	3 or 2
Mounted	3cm	4cm	3 or 2
Artillery	4cm	6cm	2 + gun
Horse Artillery	6cm	8cm	2 + gun & horse
Sniper(s)	2cm	3cm	1 or 2
Combat Engineers	2cm	3cm	4

The General's Command Unit will have three figures to represent a greater number of staff and support members, and sub-commanders shall have two figures.

VI. Army Point System

Constructing Armies using the point system:

Command Units:

Brilliant General	6.0
Average General	4.0
Poor General	2.0
Brilliant Sub-Command	4.0
Average Sub-Command	2.0
Poor Sub-Command	1.0

Mounted Units:

Cavalry Unit, Average	3.0
Cavalry Unit, Elite	4.0
Mounted Infantry, Add +1 to Reg. Infantry to Mount/Dismount	
Light Cavalry*	2.0

Regular Infantry Units:

Inferior	2.0
Average	2.5
Elite	3.0

(Points based upon smooth bore muskets)

Artillery:

Basic Unit	3.0
Heavy Artillery	4.0
Horse Artillery	4.0

Specialty Units:

Snipers*	1.0	Light Infantry*	1.0
Combat Engineers	1.0	Dummy Units#	0.5

* (always Average)

(Dummy Units are used to confuse an enemy during deployment. Once they are within range of the enemy's view they are removed from play.)

Modifying Unit Types:

In addition to the above points for Unit types, Units with advanced weapons and special abilities are provided for.

Following is a non-exclusive, non-exhaustive, list of point costs for advanced weapons and special abilities:

Infantry weapons that provide extra volleys, cost per extra volley:	0.5
Infantry weapons that provide extra range compared to the smooth bore musket, cost per extra 100 meters:	0.5
Artillery weapons that increases the accuracy of artillery (by using rifling for example) without necessarily increasing the range:	Count as 'Elite' +1
Artillery weapons that increase to firing rate, extra volley (such as breach loading artillery):	1.0
Artillery weapons that increase the accurate range of artillery cost per extra 500 meters:	1.0

Example: an Elite Mounted Infantry Unit armed with a Sharps Rifle with the ability to dismount and fight as Regular Infantry will cost 1 extra point for the ability to mount/dismount in battle, 0.5 extra points for each additional volleys it gets per Round (which will be 2 extra volleys for the Sharps Rifle for 1 extra point), and 0.5 extra points for each 100 meters of range in excess of 100 meters (which will be an extra 200 meters or 1 extra point). As such instead of costing 3.0 for an Elite Infantry Unit as described above, this Elite Mounted Infantry Unit armed with Sharps Rifles will cost 6.0. On the other hand, an Average Mounted Infantry Unit that has the dismount ability, but is not armed with any advanced weapons, will only cost 3 points.

Further on the issue of Mounted Infantry, unless they are armed with weapons that allow for multiple volleys from horse back they must dismount and fight on foot. If they are armed with more advanced weapons allowing for multiple volley then they can remain mounted, but still fight as Regular Infantry in regard to shooting and melee.

Players should feel free to add additional modifications as they see fit. There are far too many weapons types during this period to include here.

VII. Combat Rules

INITIAL DEPLOYMENT

There are many ways to initially deploy depending upon selected scenarios and the wishes of the players. Here is one traditional system that works:

1.   Both sides dice.

2.   The low scorer chooses the terrain from that available and places it on the game area. The lower scorer now can either flip a coin to determine which side he gets, or roll a die.

3.   The low scorer deploys all his Units within 1000 meters (10 cm) of his base edge or if it is a shore line the water's edge. All the Units will be placed face down. Then the high scorer deploys all his Units in the same manner.

Optional Cards for Deployment: Create a card 5 cm wide and 3 cm deep for each Unit plus additional dummy cards of up to one third of your total Units (at a cost of .5 points). Make a notation on the 'down side' of each card regarding which Unit the card represents or whether it is a dummy card. Then deploy all cards face down, or set aside as the Reserve Force if desired. When a Unit is within line of sight (see below) of an enemy force, unless obstructed by features that would leave them out of sight of the enemy, roll one d10 and on a roll of 6 to 10 the card is turned over and replaced by the actual Unit it represents unless the card was a dummy card in which case it is removed. On a roll of 1 to 5 the Unit has not been noticed by the enemy and continues on face down.

<u>What is line of sight for deployment and for movement towards the enemy?</u> 4000 meters (40 cm) in clear terrain. What could obstruct an enemy's line of sight? A dense forest, steep hill, a screen of friendly Units, or other blocking features while the card is more than 1000 meters (10 cm) from an enemy. Within 1000 meters (10 cm) all cards are turned over regardless of terrain or features.

<u>Optional Deployment of a Reserve Force</u>: A player may set aside up to one third of his Units as a Reserve Force held off the playing area. There must be at least one Sub-Command Unit included in the Reserve Force.

Different scenarios may require a different method of initial deployment. Feel free to improvise.

SEQUENCE OF PLAY

The Game is played in Rounds, and each Round is made up of the following Sequences with the High Scorer going first:

1.   Player Rolls for Initiative Points.

2.   After the first Round, if the Player has a Reserve Force and wishes to bring it onto the field he may do so by first declaring where he wishes this force to come onto the field; his base edge, his left flank, his right flank, or his enemies base edge. He then rolls a d10: a force arriving on his base edge requires a roll of 5 or higher, on either flank requires a roll of 7 or higher, or along the enemies base edge requires a roll of 9 or 10. If using cards, all Units must be placed with the cards face down within 1000 meters (10 cm) of the edge. There is no penalty for a failed attempt other than the Reserve Force does not come onto the field. Another attempt can be made during another Round.

3.   Player then moves according to the number of Initiative Points he rolled.

4.   Resolve Combat:

  ○ Those Units, on both sides, who can shoot must do so in any order desired by the Moving Player.

  ○ Units in contact enter into Melee in any order desired by the Moving Player.

5.   The above sequence is repeated by other player.

The Round is over. Repeat.

MOVEMENT

Field Movement

Movement for each player is determined by using the player's Initiative Points. For each point the player can move either a single Unit, a Command Group, a Column, or a Line. An extra point will be needed for the following circumstances:

- if the move includes artillery that is not within a Command Group.

- if all of a Unit, a Command Group, a Column or a Line is within the general's line-of-site (LOS), but more than 2,500 meters (25 cm) from the general's Unit.

- if all of a Unit, a Command Group, a Column or a Line is outside of the general's line-of-site (LOS) and more than 1,000 meters (10 cm) away.

- if the general has been lost.

Command Group – A Command Group is composed of any and all Units, Columns, or Lines which are at least partially within the command range of a command Unit such as a General or a Sub-Command at the beginning of the Round. The command range is measured from the edge of the base of the command Unit. Different Commands have different ranges:

- A Brilliant General has a command range 1,500 meters (15 cm).

- An Average General or a Brilliant Sub-Command has a command range of 1,000 meters (10 cm).

- An Inferior General or an Average Sub-Command has a command range of 500 meters (5 cm).

- An Inferior Sub-Command must be in actual contact with the Units, Columns or Lines in order for them to be considered part of its Command Group.

Each Unit within the Command Group can make individual moves independently from other Units in the Command Group as part of the single initiative point for the Command Group.

Column – A Column is composed of at least two Units formed one base width wide directly in contact behind one another at the beginning of the Round. A Column can be composed of different troop types, but may not include Snipers and/or Combat Engineers.

<u>Line</u> – A Line is composed of no less than three combat Units of the same type (other than artillery, Snipers and/or Combat Engineers which cannot form a line) formed in a line contacting Unit to Unit, front base corner to front base corner, facing in the same direction at the beginning of the Round. Units formed into a Line must move parallel to, or follow the first of them that moves, and must move the same distance or wheel through the same angles. Each Unit in a Line must cross a river individually unless part of a Command Unit.

<u>Movement by Single Unit</u> – A move by a single Unit, alone or as part of a Command Group can be in any direction as long as no part of the base moves more than the movement allowance of the Unit unless the Unit is in contact with an enemy to its front and to its flank or rear in which case the Unit will be unable to move.

<u>Miscellaneous Movement Issues</u> -

- No Unit can move across the Zone of Control of an enemy Unit, which is an area 500 meters (5 cm) directly in front of the enemy Unit and not separated from it by another Unit, other than to advance upon the enemy Unit's front or to retire directly to the rear without deviation.

- Snipers may ignore enemy Zones of Control.

- Artillery can never move into contact with an enemy, and cannot move in bad going.

- Infantry may not move into contact with any mounted.

- Snipers and Combat Engineers cannot move into contact with any enemy.

Movement allotment for Units

2000 meters	20 cm	if Light Cavalry in good going.
1000 meters	10 cm	if Cavalry or Command Unit in good going; if any other troops moving by road.
500 meters	5 cm	if Snipers regardless of terrain; if Mounted in bad going; if Horse Artillery in good going; if Infantry in Column.
300 meters	3 cm	if Infantry and Combat Engineers in good going;
200 meters	2 cm	if Artillery in good going; if Infantry and Combat Engineers in bad going; if any Unit crossing a river
100 meters	1 cm	if Heavy Artillery in good going
NOTE:		* Disordered Units may not move but can only reform. * Artillery cannot move into bad going, and therefore has no movement allotment in bad going.

Subsequent Movement

Some mounted troops get a subsequent movement if the Player has enough Initiative Points, and the subsequent movement would result in contact with enemy troops. Cavalry can move up to an additional one half (1/2) of its movement, and Light Cavalry can move up to an additional full movement if this results in contact with the enemy. This is intended to equate to a cavalry charge.

Mounting/Dismounting Mounted Infantry

Mounted Infantry can mount/dismount during combat. A Unit mounting/dismounting has used its movement for the Round and may not move further during the turn.

Reorder after Disorder

Any Unit that is in Disorder can Reorder itself at a cost of one Initiative Point per Unit per turn. After the Unit is reordered, the disorder marker is removed, and the Unit has concluded its movement for the Round.

Crossing Rivers

Rivers are an unknown. Neither player knows exactly what the condition of the river is until he attempts a crossing. When the first Unit attempts to cross a river during the game, except at a road ford or bridge, the player will roll a d10 to determine the condition of the river.

- A score of 7 to 10 indicates that it is too shallow to aid in defense and has no effect on movement; in other words for purposes of the game the river does not really exit.

- A score 1 to 3 indicates the river is a difficult river to cross, and that each Unit crossing except at a road ford or bridge must roll separately and score 6 or more to cross regardless of formation or Command Unit support.

- A score of a 4 to 6 indicates that the river is a normal river. It will aid in defense, and will not change movement rates.

A Difficult or Normal River will be considered "bad going" in all respects except for 'Combat Modifiers'. A Unit defending a river bank gets a +1 to its die roll, and the attacking Unit should not get a -2 modifier for being in "bad going". If both Units in combat are in the river neither Unit should receive the negative modifier for being in "bad going". Although the river should not be treated as "bad going" in regards to the 'Combat Modifier', it should be treated as "bad going" in regards to the 'Combat Outcome Chart'.

Moving Through Friendly Troops

Mounted, Light Infantry, Sniper, and Engineer Units can pass through Command Units, and all Units can move through Sniper and Engineer Units.

Combat Engineering

If a Player has Combat Engineers, he may choose to use them to build roads, and build field fortifications to provide support and defenses to combat Units. No construction can continue if there is an enemy Units within 500 meters of the Combat Engineer unless the enemy is at least partially screened off by friendly troops. Each Combat Engineer Unit can build or demolish 200 meters of roads, 100 meters of a bridge that crosses a river, or 200 meters of field fortifications per turn.

The successful completion of a bridge over a river means that all movement and combat modifiers for that river are removed for Units using the bridge.

A Combat Engineer that has moved cannot construct or demolish during that turn. Please note that field fortifications have no effect on movement, but only upon combat.

COMBAT

Combat includes Shooting and Melee.

NOTE: Snipers and Combat Engineers do not have fronts, sides and rears like other Units. For Snipers, every edge is treated as a "front" for Shooting and a "rear" for Melee, and for Combat Engineers every edge is a "rear" for all Combats. As such Snipers may shoot in any direction since every direction is straight ahead, and Combat Engineers cannot initiate shooting since they have no "straight ahead" but may return fire if shot at by an enemy Unit. In regards to Melee, neither Unit can be contacted in the flank or rear as described for other Units, but additional Units in contact will be treated as overlaps. Since neither Snipers nor Combat Engineers have "fronts" for Melee the attacking player gets to choose which Unit is the primary attacker if there are more than one Unit in contact.

Shooting

Units with the ability to shoot can and must shoot at any one enemy Unit within a base width of straight ahead (or in other words a 1500 meter wide area straight ahead) and within its range, but only if neither is in Melee or overlapping another Unit in Melee, and no other Unit is between them as measured from the center of the shooting Unit to the center of the target Unit.

Range of Weapons

Where possible, troop types will remain the same, but their weapons will vary in range and rate of fire. As such a Unit that is armed with a more "advanced" weapon fighting against a similar Unit with a less "advanced" weapon will only have an advantage when firing. In Melee, unless specifically stated otherwise, there will be no advantage or disadvantage.

Artillery	1500 meters
Heavy Artillery	2400 meters
Snipers (w/ Rifles)	500 meters
Advanced Rifles (may vary)	300 meters
Rifled Muskets	200 meters
Smooth-Bore Muskets	100 meters
Other ballistic weapons such as pistols, bows, etc.	50 meters

NOTE: This is a very limited table and can be supplemented in customized lists. Weapons with a rapid rate of fire will be able to fire more than once during a player's turn, such ability to be referred to as a Multiple Volley (examples: the breach loading Sharps Rifle, Martini-Henri Rifles, or perhaps even more so for Gatling Guns and other "machine guns" of the era).

A target that has not already shot and which can shoot back must do so. Artillery shoots only if it did not move during the Round, but can shoot if it has only pivoted. Also, if Artillery is located on elevated terrain, it may shoot over friendly troops into enemy troops as long as friendly troops are more than 400 meters away from the target.

All of the above is of course subject to Line of Site (LOS) limitations. Shooting Units cannot fire through or above LOS obstacles such as trees, BUA, etc. However, Units in a LOS obstacle can shoot out of these areas into open areas.

Except for the opponents not being in contact and some shooting being un-returned, the effects of shooting are resolved exactly as described below in Combat. A 2nd or 3rd Unit that shoots at the same target Unit aids the shooting of the primary Unit instead of being treated separately.

A Unit being shot at does not turn to face the opponent if being shot at from the flank or rear (otherwise known as "enfilading fire"). A Unit is being hit with enfilading fire when the firing Unit or a supporting firing Unit is shooting the flank or rear of a target Unit, and at least 50% of the firing Unit is behind the front line of the target Unit (or in other words the center line of the firing Unit is in line with or behind the front line of the target Unit).

Melee

Melee occurs when a Unit has moved into, or remains in, both front edge and corner to corner base contact with an enemy Unit. A Unit not in frontal contact which is contacted to flank or rear by an enemy front edge turns to face at the end of the movement phase. If a Unit contacts the flanks of two such enemy Units, both these turn, the second moving behind the first.

When a Unit is attacked in flank or rear while also in contact with an enemy to its front, only one set of dice are used based upon the combat factor of the Unit to its front, and the other Units act as negative modifiers for the defending Unit. If the defending Unit wins, its flank and rear opponents fall back regardless of the outcome for the Unit in frontal contact. If it loses, it is destroyed unless outcome indicates a hold. A Unit cannot be overlapped and contacted on the same flank, or be overlapped by an enemy unless both right or both left corners or any side edges touch. Opposing Units in mutual edge contact overlap each other. A Unit can count as an overlap against two enemy elements on opposite flanks, or against Units exposed by its frontal opponents having fallen back, fled or been destroyed that Round.

Combat Outcome

Whether Shooting or in Melee, <u>both players roll two (2) dice</u> to determine the outcome of combat using the COMBAT CHART.

For Inferior Units use 2d6, for Average Units use 2d8, and for Elite Units us 2d10.

A Unit which scores less than that of its opponent must react as described below in the COMBAT OUTCOME CHART, except for Units which shoot without being shot back (which includes Units which have only provided shooting support or overlap) which disregard an unfavorable outcome. Please note that a Unit that has provided rear support, is in contact to the flank, or is in contact to the rear in a Melee will not suffer the same outcome as the Unit it is supporting which is in front edge contact with an enemy Unit, but in the case of a Unit supporting from the rear will fall back without rolling for casualties if the front Unit falls back, will flee in disorder without rolling for casualties if the front Unit flees, and will flee in disorder and roll for casualties if the front Unit is destroyed while a Unit in contact with the flank or rear of an enemy will simply fall back without rolling for casualties.

Understand 'Quick Kills', and Flank and Rear Attacks – A 'Quick Kill' is the ability of one type of Unit to completely destroy another type of Unit in Combat if it is able to double the other Unit's score or in some cases merely beat it without doubling the score. This is very important to understand. Study the outcome table to better understand which Units are more vulnerable to other Units. For instance, Infantry can only be 'Quick Killed' by a Mounted Unit in frontal contact if the Mounted Unit scores double.

The other way to destroy an enemy Unit is to attack from the front, and also attack the enemy Unit's flank or rear. This guarantees the destruction of the Unit if your score beats the enemy Unit but does not double it since the Unit can no longer fall back or flee. Watch your flanks and rear!

So if your goal is to destroy an opposing Infantry Unit there are only two ways to do it: 1. Use a Mounted Unit in a frontal attack if you think the circumstance makes it possible for you to double the score of the Infantry Unit, or 2. In addition to the frontal attack, you also place a Unit in contact with the enemies flank or rear.

COMBAT CHART

Unit Shooting	vs	Inf.	Mounted
Regular Infantry		+4	+2
Combat Engineers		+1	+0
Light Infantry		+2	+1
Infantry in Disorder		+1	+0
Command Unit		+1	+1
Cavalry		+2	+2
Light Cavalry		+1	+1
Mounted in Disorder		+1	+0
Snipers		+2	+1
Artillery – more than 500 meters		+3	+2
Artillery – 500 meters or less		+7	+4

Unit in Melee	vs	Inf.	Mounted
Regular Infantry		+2	+2
Combat Engineers		+1	+1
Light Infantry		+1	+1
Infantry in Disorder		+1	+0
Command Unit		+1	+1
Cavalry		+4	+3
Light Cavalry		+1	+2
Mounted in Disorder		+2	+1
Snipers		-2	+0
Artillery		+2	+2

Positive Modifiers

+1 if enfilading fire

+1 if the General's Unit in Melee

+1 if in Melee and either uphill or defending a river bank except at a road ford or bridge

+1 if in Melee or Shooting from a completed field fortification

+1 If Heavy Artillery

+1 For each extra Infantry Volley

Negative Modifiers

-1 for each flank overlapped, for each enemy element in contact with flank or rear, for each 2nd or 3rd Unit aiding a shooting enemy, or for a Unit of Regular Infantry behind another Regular Infantry Unit attacking to the front.

-1 for each casualty suffered

-2 if in, or mounted in contact with enemy in, bad going on or off-road, except Snipers and Light Infantry.

COMBAT OUTCOME CHART

If the losing Unit is not DOUBLED:

-<u>Regular Infantry (Incl Light Inf)</u> if in contact against Mounted, flee in disorder and roll for casualties. Otherwise fall back and roll for casualties.

-<u>Command Unit</u> if in contact flee in disorder and roll for casualties. Otherwise fall back.

-<u>Reg Mounted</u> fall back, if in bad going fall back and roll for casualties.

-<u>Light Cavalry</u> fall back, unless in bad going then flee in disorder.

-<u>Inf or Mtd in Disorder</u> flee in disorder and roll for casualties.

-<u>Snipers</u> disregard negative outcomes from shooting; flee if in contact.

-<u>Combat Engineers</u> if in contact destroyed, otherwise flee.

-<u>Artillery</u> if being shot at roll for casualties. If in contact destroyed.

If the losing Unit is DOUBLED:

-<u>Regular Infantry (Incl Light Inf)</u> if in contact against Mounted destroyed. Otherwise flee in disorder and roll for casualties.

-<u>Command Unit</u> if in contact destroyed. Otherwise flee in disorder and roll for casualties.

-<u>Reg Mounted</u> if in contact against Mounted or in bad going destroyed. Otherwise flee in disorder and roll for casualties.

-<u>Light Cavalry</u> if in contact with Mounted, flee in disorder and roll for casualties. Otherwise flee in disorder.

-<u>Inf or Mtd in Disorder</u> destroyed.

-<u>Snipers</u> disregard negative outcomes from shooting; destroyed if in contact.

-<u>Combat Engineers</u> destroyed.

-<u>Artillery</u> if being shot at roll for casualties twice, after that destroyed.

Rolling for Casualties

Where indicated in the outcome tables above, the losing player must roll a 1d6 to see if the Unit suffers a single casualty. A roll of 1 to 3 indicates that the Unit suffered a single casualty. Some indication must be made that the Unit suffered a casualty (a colored rubberband, etc.). Please note that a casualty does not necessarily correspond to a specific number of soldiers, but is an abstract representation of loss of effectiveness of the Unit. The 'casualty' will result in a negative modifier of -1 against it in any combat rolls.

Movement After Combat

A Unit which must "fall back" moves back 3 cm to its rear without turning. If it meets friends who are facing in the same direction, it passes through to their rear if it is allowed to do so, otherwise it pushes back any but artillery. Troops not facing in the same direction cannot be passed through or pushed back with the exception of Snipers and Engineers which can always be passed through. A Unit which must fall back in contact with enemy to both front and flank or rear, or that meets enemy, or terrain it cannot cross, friends that it cannot pass through or push back, is destroyed.

A fleeing Unit falls back 3 cm then turns 180 degrees and moves its full movement allowance in that direction. It changes direction only by the minimum amount necessary to avoid enemy, friends it cannot pass through, or bad or impassable going, but not to avoid crossing a river. If the Unit is blocked by enemy

Units, friendly Units it cannot pass through or bad or impassable terrain, it is destroyed. Failure to cross a river results in the Unit being destroyed. After the Unit flees, it is in Disorder. A fleeing Unit can pass through any gap between friendly Units and/or bad or impassable terrain in order to complete its movement regardless of how small the gap.

The exception to the above is the Sniper who will "flee" through any gap or hole regardless of how small which may include the space between enemy Units. A Sniper cannot be "cornered" by being surrounded by enemy Units even if enemy Units are in corner to corner contact surrounding the Sniper. The Sniper will always be able to flee in the direction of its choice if the Combat Outcome provides for such.

When a Unit is destroyed in combat any Unit 500 meters (5 cm) to the rear are forced to flee in disorder and roll for casualties.

VIII. Winning and Losing

The first side that at the end of any Round has lost 15 points (or whatever level the Players agree upon), and has also lost more points than the enemy, loses the battle. Elements that recoil or flee from the board edge are counted as lost, although they may reappear in the next Round if playing a campaign.

Appendix

These lists are just samples of what can be done using the Army Point System in Section VI. They are not intended to be exhaustive or conclusive. In fact I don't even want to describe these lists as 'suggested' as I am not confident enough to do that. Please feel free to create your own weapons modifications where you think they are needed, change those you disagree with, and please share those modifications on the website:

http://www.bozbat.com/

Weapons Modifications and Supplemental Rules

Infantry Weapons

Supplemental Rules for Machine Guns

In these lists various machine guns are included as Infantry Weapons, and treated as a type of artillery with more limited range for combat.

Perhaps instead they should be treated as infantry with a greatly enhanced Positive Modifier in the Combat Chart, or perhaps the defending unit should receive a Negative Modifier when facing a machine gun unit?

- Arisaka Type 30 Rifle – was the standard-issue rifle of Japan during the early 1900s. It was a bolt-action rifle with a 5-round magazine and a caliber of 6.5mm. +4 Extra Volleys, +3 100m.

- Chassepot Rifle 1866 (France) – The Chassepot rifle, also known as the Fusil Modèle 1866, was a bolt-action rifle that was used by the French Army during the mid-to-late 19th century. It was a significant advancement in firearms technology and played a prominent role in several conflicts of the time, including the Franco-Prussian War. +1 Extra Volleys, +2 100m.

- Colt–Browning M1895 – The Colt-Browning M1895 was an air-cooled, belt-fed, gas-operated machine gun based on an 1889 design by John Browning and his brother Matthew. It is nicknamed "potato digger" due to its unusual operating mechanism and fires from a closed bolt with a cyclic rate of 450 rounds per minute. Treat as artillery with only a range of 500m.

- Dreyse Needle Gun (Prussia) – This revolutionary weapon, invented in 1836, was the first breach-loading rifle to use the bolt action mechanism. The real advantage of the Dreyse was its speed of reloading, and the ability of the soldier to load it while lying down perhaps behind cover. +1 Extra Volleys, +1 100m.

- French M1853/67 Infantry rifles "à Tabatière" – Actually a collection of various rifled muskets converted to breach-loaders. The 'tabatiere' refers to the shape of the breach mechanism which looked a bit like a snuff box. +1 Extra Volley, +1 100m.

- French Model 1822 Fusil de Arisco: This was a flintlock muzzle-loading, smoothbore musket used by by France in many conflicts, and was standard issue for Mexico during the Mexican-American War.

- Gatling Gun – The Gatling gun is an early type of machine gun that was invented by Richard Gatling in the mid-19th century. It was one of the first practical rapid-firing firearms, capable of firing multiple rounds per minute, and represented a significant advancement in firepower compared to traditional firearms of its time. The Gatling gun featured a hand-cranked, multi-barrel design. It typically had six to ten barrels that were mounted around a central axis and could rotate as the gun was hand-cranked. As the barrels rotated, cartridges were loaded into the breech of each barrel from a hopper, and the firing mechanism discharged the cartridges one at a time as each barrel reached the firing position. This allowed for continuous fire as long as the hand-crank was turned, making it a highly effective and rapid-firing weapon for its time. Treat as artillery with only a range of 500m.

- Hotchkiss Machine Gun – The Hotchkiss was an air-cooled belt fed machine gun designed by Benjamin B. Hotchkiss, an American engineer and inventor, in the late 19th century. It was known for its simplicity, reliability, and effectiveness. Treat as artillery with only a range of 500m.

- Kammerlader M1849 (Norway) – +1 Extra Volley, +2 100m.

- Lee-Enfield – The Lee-Enfield is a family of bolt-action magazine fed rifles that were the standard service rifles of the British Empire and Commonwealth during the late 19th and early 20th centuries. +4 Extra Volleys, +3 100m.

- Mauser – The Mauser is a family of bolt-action magazine fed rifles that were developed by the German arms manufacturer Mauser-Werke, and became widely known for their high-quality, accurate, and reliable designs. +4 Extra Volleys, +3 100m.

- Maxim (Machine) Gun – Hiram Stevens Maxim of the United States is credited with inventing the Maxim machine gun (c. 1884), which **utilized smokeless gunpowder to convert hand-cranked machine guns into truly automatic weapons by harnessing the recoil so as to work the bolt, expel the spent cartridge, and reload.** Treat as artillery with only a range of 500m.

- Minie Rifle – Pattern 1851 (France) – +1 100m.

- M1870 Berdan – The Berdan was a breech-loading, single-shot rifle that used metallic cartridges. It had a very long range and was known for it accuracy. +2 Extra Volleys, +3 100m.

- M1870 Peabody-Martini – The Peabody-Martini was a breech-loading, single-shot rifle that used metallic cartridges. It had a very long range and was known for it accuracy. +2 Extra Volleys, +3 100m.

- Martini-Henry Rifle – The Martini-Henry rifle was designed by Friedrich von Martini, a Swiss engineer, and Alexander Henry, a Scottish gunsmith. It was introduced as the standard infantry rifle in the British forces in 1871, and featured a falling block action, where the breech block was hinged and dropped down to allow for loading and extraction of the cartridge. The rifle was chambered for the .577/450 Martini-Henry cartridge, which was a large-caliber round with ferocious stopping power. +2 Extra Volleys, +2 100m.

- Model 1819 Hall Rifle – A breech-loading, single-shot, bolt action rifle using metal cartridge system deployed in small numbers by the United States during the Mexican-American War. It was a significant technological advancement, but was not adopted by the US military. +2 Extra Volleys, +2 100m.

- Model 1841 Mississippi Rifle – This was a muzzle-loading, single-shot rifle used by the United States during the Mexican-American War. It had a caliber of .54 inches and featured a longer barrel with deeper rifling, which increased accuracy and range. +2 100m.

- Model 1842 Springfield Musket – This was a muzzle-loading, smoothbore musket used by the United States during the Mexican-American War, various Indian conflicts, and in limited use during the American Civil War. Although it was not rifled, its use of standardized paper cartridges which improved loading/reloading. +1 Extra Volley.

- Mosin-Nagant Model 1891 – The Mosin-Nagant was the standard-issue rifle for the Russian and then Soviet army up until World War II. It was a 5-round magazine-fed rifle with a caliber of 7.62mm. +4 Extra Volleys, +3 100m.

- Pattern 1831 British Brunswick Rifle – This was a muzzle-loading, single-shot rifle adopted by the British in 1837. It was used by the British in various conflicts including the Crimean War, and in limited numbers by the Mexicans during the Mexican-American War. It was phased out in the 1850s. It had a caliber of .704 inches and featured rifling with six shallow grooves. The Brunswick Rifle was known for its accuracy. +1 100.

- Sharps Rifle (aka Sharps Carbine) – The Sharps Rifle was patented in 1841, and went into serious production in the 1850s. It was a breach loading rifle that was extraordinarily accurate with a long range. Various improvements made it an ideal weapon for cavalry and snipers during the American Civil War. +2 Extra Volleys, +2 100m.

- Winchester Model 1894 –The Winchester Model 1894 is a lever-action repeating rifle that was introduced by the Winchester Repeating Arms Company in 1894. It became one of the most popular and iconic rifles in American history, known for its compact size, durability, and versatility. +3 Extra Volleys, +2 100m.

Artillery

- Austrian 8-pounder Rifled Breech-Loading Artillery – These cannons were available to the Austrians during the Austro-Prussian War, but seemed to play a minor role due to other problems in the Austrian military. Basic Artillery cost (+ 3) +1 Extra Volleys, +2 for Extra Range (+1,000m), and +1 for greater Accuracy; total cost +7 per unit.

- Austrian M.1863 4-pounder – The standard artillery of the Austrian military preceding and during the Austro-Prussian War, this rifled muzzle-loading cannon was efficient, accurate, and effective. Treat as 'Elite' Basic Artillery +1.

- 3" Ordnance Rifle – An extremely accurate rifled muzzle loaded cannon made of cast iron used by both the USA and the Confederacy in the American Civil War. It was a rugged and durable, and increased the accuracy the cannon more than the range although there was a marginal increase. Perhaps the best way to deal with these pieces would be to treat them as 'Elite' Basic Artillery, add +1 in cost, and otherwise treat them as Basic Artillery.

- James Rifle (USA) – A standard bronze 6-pounder muzzle loading cannon modified with rifling. As with the 3" Ordnance Rifle, it improved accuracy more than range. Treat it in the same manner as the 3" Ordnance Rifle.

- Parrot Guns (ACW) – Both the USA and the Confederacy used these cast iron rifled cannons. They came in 'Basic' as well as 'Heavy' type artillery. They were more accurate, but came at the cost of lower safety and reliability. Like the 3" Ordnance Rifle, it improved accuracy rather than range.

- Whitworth Breech-Loading Rifle (12-pounder) – Made in Britain and one of the first 'modern' artillery. It combined breach loading with rifling making it faster to load and fire, more accurate, and with increased range. It was ideal for counter artillery-battery fire. Basic Artillery cost (+ 3) +1 Extra Volleys, +2 for Extra Range (+1,000m), and +1 for greater Accuracy; total cost +7 per unit.

Cars and Trains

Movement – Treat cars as Cavalry for movement in 'good going', and in 'bad going' they can only move if they roll a 5 or 6 on a 6 sided die and then move as Cavalry – a failed roll still is treated as a move for initiative points. Trains are limited to the tracks of the railroad which are always 'good going' unless obstructed, and are treated as Light Cavalry for movement.

Combat – In combat cars and trains are treated as Engineers with no ability to shoot unless artillery or machine guns are mounted on them in some manner – then they are treated as the weapons mounted when in combat. For instance, Infantry if loaded aboard a train, will be treated like the type of infantry in question.

Airplanes and Balloons

Rules for Airplanes and Balloons:

1. Movement and Range:

   Airplanes – 3000m to 4000m depending upon the speed of the airplane, and an altitude of no more than 750m. Should be deployed off the board unless the airfield is part of the battle field.

   Balloons – Normally tethered to the ground, but if allowed to float freely, or if the tether is cut for some reason, they will be taken by the wind. Roll an 8 sided die to determine wind direction – 1 North, 2 Northeast, 3 East, 4 Southeast, 5 South, 6 Southwest, 7 West, and 8 Northwest, and then roll a 6 sided die for speed – 1, 2, or 3 Zero, 4 100m, 5 200m, and 6 300m.

2. Line of Sight: Most aircraft during the period covered in this game were used primarily for reconnaissance due to their elevated vantage point and extended line of sight. However, with the absence of radios they would have to fly back and deliver the information or perhaps drop a canister with the information near the HQ.

3. Combat Abilities: Some aircraft could drop bombs, but the impact was more psychological than physical – bombing could occasionally result in hysterical responses from unprepared enemies. If the airplane can drop bombs treat them like Light Cavalry shooting in the Combat Tables with the defenders unable to shoot back. Perhaps have the attacking aircraft treated as Elite (Light Cavalry) and the defenders as Inferior regardless of troop type, and allow the defenders to shoot. There is no air to air combat.

4. Damage and Resilience: Aircraft and balloons may be vulnerable to small arms fire if within range, and in the case of balloons if the position they are tethered to is taken they could be cut loose or worse.

5. Command and Control: Aircraft are given written orders and then once in the air all contact is lost. Each turn the player should roll a 6 sided die and if the result is 1 or 2 the airplane does not move. If the player rolls 1 or 2 two times in a row the airplane must make an emergency landing within 2000m of its current position.

- Blériot XI: This was a French-designed aircraft used by the Ottoman Empire for reconnaissance and observation missions. It was a single-engine monoplane with a wingspan of around 8 meters and had a top speed of around 80 km/h.

- Etrich Taube: This was an Austrian-designed aircraft used by Italy in the early 20th Century for reconnaissance and observation missions. It was a biplane with a distinctive bird-like appearance, featuring a monocoque fuselage and a wingspan of around 11 meters.

- Farman MF.11: This was a French-designed aircraft used by Italy for reconnaissance and observation missions in the early 20th Century. It was a biplane with a wingspan of around 14 meters and had a top speed of around 85 km/h.

- Nieuport IV.G: This was a French-designed aircraft used by Italy in the early 20th Century for bombing missions. It was a single-engine monoplane with a top speed of around 100 km/h and carried a small bomb load.

- Rumpler Taube: This was a German-designed aircraft used by the Ottoman Empire for reconnaissance and observation missions. It was a biplane with a wingspan of around 10 meters and had a top speed of around 100 km/h.

- Voisin 1910: This was a French-designed aircraft used by the Ottoman Empire for reconnaissance and observation missions. It was a biplane with a wingspan of around 13 meters and had a top speed of around 80 km/h.

Historical Conflicts and Some Sample Army Lists

Initially I did not want to come up with army lists, or even suggestions, because each army from each conflict would/should possibly qualify for their own book rather than a brief summary and perhaps some sample lists. I am imagining the hate mail I will receive for each over-simplification or error I make. I also do not believe I have the expertise to attempt such a monumental task. Just the differences between the weapons of the Franco-Prussian and Russo-Turkish wars provide a dramatic example of how profound the differences can be.

As such, I am providing these descriptions and lists with a profound sense of unease. I know my knowledge of the history, technology, and tactics of the period is inadequate. However, I am not sure anyone else could do any better, so I will offer these lists with a humble request for patience and tolerance. If you see something that is incorrect in any way please change it in your games, and contact me to correct me. I look forward to and in fact depend upon such corrections.

I will include a brief description of conflict where I think it is appropriate, comments on the weapons if useful, and comments that I think might be useful. Lists are sorted in Alphabetical Order.

American Civil War (1861 – 1865)

The American Civil War began when the Southern States seceded from the United States of America and formed the Confederacy. After failed negotiations the remaining states of the USA, often referred to as the North or the Union, began a war to return the seceding states to the USA.

Since the American Civil War is perhaps one of the most well known and comprehensively chronicled wars of the period I will not attempt more of a description.

Nor will I attempt army lists since an entire book could be written on that topic, and in fact has.

I will point out that cavalry was used differently than in past conflicts, and in most European armies. In general USA and Confederate cavalry did not charge (although there are some examples where they did charge). As such I think most, if not all such cavalry, should be treated as Mounted Infantry with the ability to mount/dismount and fight on foot. Perhaps if armed with appropriate weapons that provided for multiple volleys such units could fight mounted as Regular Infantry for shooting and melee giving them greater maneuverability, but could not 'charge' into melee as Cavalry.

Both USA and Confederate armies started the war off with rifled muskets (+200 m): each infantry unit should add +1 point.

Although there were some interesting experiments in more advanced weaponry on the Confederate side, they lacked the industrial base for mass production. The USA on the other hand developed and produced more advanced weapons from small arms to artillery. The Confederacy did import some interesting new weaponry, particularly from the British.

The USA had an advantage in Heavy Artillery whereas most Confederate artillery was Basic Artillery.

Austro-Prussian War (1866)

The Austro-Prussian War started as a seemingly trivial dispute between two equal powers, Prussia and Austria, over a minor province that both parties had agreed to co-rule, and became a conflict between Prussia and Italy against Austria. After about seven weeks of fighting Prussia and its allies became the dominant power block in Central Europe.

The Austrians failed to recognize the disadvantages they faced against the Prussian alliance. The Prussians had developed one of the first modern national armies based upon universal conscription and a sophisticated reserve system, while the Austrians had a rather haphazard military system that often failed to even honor its own rules; commanders would often send conscripted soldiers back home rather than bother to train them. Also, the Austrians often viewed their own military made up of a polyglot of ethnic groups as a greater threat than foreign enemies.

The Prussians also had an advantage in logistics with a larger and more advanced railway system giving them the ability to better mobilize, move and supply its armies.

In regards to armaments, the Prussians had the superior breach-loading Dreyse Needle Guns against the Austrian Lorenz Rifles which were sturdy but slow muzzle loading rifled muskets, but the Austrians had a modest number of advanced breach-loading rifled artillery against the Prussians who made do with old model muzzle-loading smooth-bore cannons.

The war began in the last week of June with inconclusive battles between the Prussian block and Austria and its allies. However, on July 3, 1866, the outnumbered Prussian army decisively defeated the Austrians effectively ending the war in Prussia's favor. The Austrian army and navy did much better against the Italians, but gained no real advantage since being defeated by the Prussians forced the Austrians to concede the province of Veneto (Venice) to the Italians.

The outcome of the war made Prussia the preeminent German power and excluded the angry and resentful Austria from further German political participation.

Boxer Rebellion (1899 – 1901)

The Boxer Rebellion was a violent anti-foreign and anti-Christian uprising that took place in China from 1899 to 1901. It was led by a secret society called the "Society of Righteous and Harmonious Fists," which became known as the Boxers due to their martial arts practices. The Boxers sought to expel foreign influence and missionaries from China, and their activities were primarily focused on attacking foreign diplomats, missionaries, and Chinese Christians.

One of the key factors that distinguished the Boxer Rebellion was the use of traditional Chinese martial arts techniques by the Boxers, which they believed made them invulnerable to foreign bullets. They would perform rituals and wear charms in the belief that it would protect them from harm, leading them to believe they were impervious to bullets. This led to the Boxers engaging in daring and reckless acts of violence against foreign diplomats, missionaries, and Chinese Christians.

The Boxers also employed guerrilla warfare tactics, such as ambushes, hit-and-run attacks, and sieges. They targeted foreign legations and settlements, resulting in a prolonged siege of the foreign legations in Beijing, which lasted for 55 days. During the siege, the Boxers utilized improvised weapons, such as spears, swords, and other traditional Chinese weapons, as well as firearms and artillery obtained from sympathetic Chinese military forces.

On the other side, the foreign forces, including troops from eight nations known as the Eight-Nation Alliance, which included the United States, United Kingdom, Japan, France, Germany, Russia, Italy, and Austria-Hungary, used modern military tactics and weaponry. They employed machine guns, artillery, and modern rifles such as the Lee Enfield and the Mauser, as well as naval bombardments, to suppress the Boxer Rebellion. The foreign forces eventually lifted the siege of the legations and quelled the uprising, resulting in significant casualties on both sides.

The Boxer Rebellion was a significant event in Chinese history, marking a period of internal turmoil and foreign intervention in China, which had long-lasting effects on Chinese society and politics. It highlighted the clash between traditional Chinese culture and modern Western influences, and the use of different weapons and tactics by the Boxers and the foreign forces reflected the technological disparities and cultural conflicts of the time.

Crimean War (1853 – 1856)

The Crimean War was a military conflict between Russia and a coalition of Great Britain, France, the Kingdom of Sardinia, and the Ottoman Empire. The conflict originated from the "Eastern Question" – what will happen to Ottoman Empire and its many possessions as it becomes ever weaker.

Since the late 18th century, Russia took advantage of this the Ottoman weakness to increase its influence around the Black Sea, and in the Balkans. Perhaps Russia even wanted to capture the Dardanelles which connect the Black Sea to the Mediterranean Sea and would give Russia access to a warm water ports on the Mediterranean.

Franco-Prussian War (1870 – 1871)

The Franco-Prussian War was a conflict that took place from 1870 to 1871 between the French Empire, led by

Napoleon III, and the Kingdom of Prussia, under the leadership of Chancellor Otto von Bismarck. The war resulted in the defeat of France and the eventual unification of Germany under Prussian dominance.

One of the notable features of the Franco-Prussian War was the use of new weapons and tactics by Prussia, which contributed to their military success. These included:

1. Needle Guns: Both France and Prussia utilized rifled breech-loading needle guns; the Chassepot rifle for the French and the Dreyse needle gun for the Prussians. Both had a significant advantage over the muzzle-loading rifles. However, the Prussian rifle had a somewhat faster rate of fire if not greater range giving Prussian troops an edge in individual firepower during engagements – although some have suggested that the Prussian advantage was due to better tactical use rather than technical superiority of the Dreyse.

2. Railways: Prussia effectively utilized railways to mobilize their troops and transport supplies, allowing for rapid deployment and concentration of forces. This strategic use of railways provided Prussia with a significant logistical advantage and helped them achieve operational superiority on the battlefield.

3. Krupp Artillery: Prussia used advanced artillery developed by the Krupp Company, including steel breech-loading cannons, which had longer range,

greater accuracy, and faster reloading times compared to the bronze muzzle-loading cannons used by the French. Krupp artillery was instrumental in breaking French defenses and achieving battlefield dominance.

4. Moltke's Operational Strategy: Prussia employed the operational strategy developed by its Chief of General Staff, Helmuth von Moltke, known as the "Moltke System." This strategy emphasized rapid mobilization, concentration of forces, and flexible maneuvering to achieve decisive victories. It allowed Prussia to swiftly defeat the French armies in a series of battles, leading to their ultimate victory.

5. Siege Warfare: Prussia effectively used siege warfare tactics, including encirclement and blockades, to besiege and capture French fortresses, such as Metz and Paris. These tactics, combined with the superior firepower of Prussian artillery, led to the defeat and capitulation of French forces.

The use of new weapons, tactics, and strategies by Prussia in the Franco-Prussian War demonstrated the importance of technological advancements and innovative military approaches in shaping the outcome of conflicts during that time. Prussia's military superiority in terms of weaponry, logistics, and strategy played a crucial role in their victory over France and the eventual unification of Germany under Prussian leadership.

Greek War of Independence (1821 – 1832)

The Greek War of Independence, also known as the Greek Revolution, was a conflict that took place from 1821 to 1832, during which Greece sought to gain independence from the Ottoman Empire. It was a significant event in modern Greek history, resulting in the establishment of the modern Greek state.

The Greek War of Independence was characterized by the use of various weapons and tactics by both the Greek revolutionaries and the Ottoman Empire. Some of the notable weapons and tactics used during the conflict include:

1. Guerrilla Warfare: The Greek revolutionaries employed guerrilla warfare tactics, including hit-and-run attacks, ambushes, and raids, against the larger and more organized Ottoman forces. Greek fighters, known as klephts and armatoloi, utilized their knowledge of the local terrain to their advantage and engaged in irregular warfare, making it difficult for the Ottoman Empire to counter their attacks.

2. Naval Warfare: The Greek revolutionaries also utilized naval warfare to gain an advantage. They established a navy comprised of small ships, known as fireships or brulots, which were loaded with explosives and set on fire before being sent towards the larger Ottoman ships. This tactic, known as "fireship warfare," was used to destroy or disable Ottoman ships and disrupt their naval operations.

3. Western Military Assistance: The Greek revolutionaries received support from other European countries, particularly France, Russia, and the United Kingdom, who provided military assistance in the form of ships, weapons, and training. This assistance helped the Greek revolutionaries in their fight for independence and provided them with access to modern weaponry and tactics.

4. Ottoman Countermeasures: The Ottoman Empire also utilized various tactics to suppress the Greek rebellion, including scorched earth policies, mass executions, and reprisals against civilian populations. They also employed regular armies and irregular forces, such as the infamous Ottoman irregular troops known as the Janissaries, to combat the Greek revolutionaries.

5. Diplomatic Efforts: The Greek revolutionaries also made diplomatic efforts to gain support from other European powers and garner international recognition for their cause. They sought diplomatic alliances and support from foreign governments to increase their chances of success in the conflict.

The Greek War of Independence was a complex and protracted conflict that involved a combination of guerrilla warfare, naval warfare, diplomatic efforts, and foreign military assistance. These various weapons and tactics used by both sides contributed to the outcome of the war, ultimately resulting in the establishment of an independent Greek state in 1832.

Italian War of 1859 (or the 2nd Italian War of Independence) (1859)

The Italian War of 1859 was fought between France and the Kingdom of Savoy-Piedmont-Sardinia (hereinafter Savoy) against Austria. In 1858 France and Savoy entered into a military agreement whereby France agreed to assist Savoy in expelling Austria from Italy. In March of 1859 Savoy mobilized its military, and Austria did the same in April. After Savoy rejected Austria's ultimatum to stand down, the war began on April 26, 1859, when Austrian forces invaded Savoy.

French forces began arriving in defense of Savoy in April and on June 4, 1859, the Austrians were defeated by the combined forces of Savoy and France at the Battle of Magenta. The Franco-Savoy forces followed up their victory with another at the Battle of Solferino delivery another defeat to the Austrians effectively ending the war.

The Austrians ceded the province of Lombardy to France which in turn ceded it to Savoy.

Weapons:

The French generally were armed with muzzle-loading rifled muskets (+1 100m), a mix of smooth bore muzzle-loading cannons and some rifled muzzle-loading cannons.

The forces of Savoy were armed with mostly smooth bore muzzle loading muskets, and the artillery were all smooth bore muzzle-loading cannons.

The Austrian forces were mostly armed with the Lorenz Rifle (see above) with about 20% armed with smooth bore muzzle-loading muskets. The Austrian artillery were mostly smooth bore muzzle-loading cannons.

Italo-Turkish War (1911 – 1912)

The Italo-Turkish War, also known as the Tripolitanian War, was a conflict that took place between Italy and the Ottoman Empire from 29 September 1911 to 18 October 1912. The war was primarily fought over the control of the Ottoman territories of Tripolitania, Cyrenaica (present-day Libya), and the Dodecanese islands in the Aegean Sea.

The Italo-Turkish War was notable for the use of various new weapons and tactics by both Italy and the Ottoman Empire. Some of the notable ones include:

1. Aircraft: The Italo-Turkish War was one of the first conflicts in which aircraft were used for military purposes. Both Italy and the Ottoman Empire utilized aircraft for reconnaissance, observation, and bombing missions. Italy, in particular, made significant use of aircraft for aerial reconnaissance and bombing of Ottoman positions, marking the first operational use of aircraft in a war.

2. Naval Warfare: Naval warfare played a significant role in the conflict, as both Italy and

the Ottoman Empire had naval forces deployed in the Mediterranean Sea. Italy utilized its modern navy, including battleships, cruisers, and destroyers, to enforce a naval blockade and support amphibious operations. The Ottoman Empire, on the other hand, relied on a smaller and outdated naval force, which was unable to effectively counter the Italian navy.

3. Mobile Warfare: Both Italy and the Ottoman Empire made use of mobile warfare tactics, including cavalry and motorized units, to conduct fast-paced operations and gain advantages in the desert and coastal regions of Tripolitania and Cyrenaica. Mobile warfare allowed for greater flexibility and maneuverability, which was essential in the challenging terrain of North Africa.

4. Siege Warfare: The Italo-Turkish War saw the use of siege warfare tactics by Italy to capture key Ottoman forts and strongholds. Italy employed artillery, including modern heavy siege guns, to bombard and breach Ottoman defenses, followed by infantry assaults to capture fortified positions.

5. Use of Colonial Troops: Italy utilized colonial troops, including indigenous soldiers from its colonies in Africa, such as Eritrea and Somalia, in the conflict. These colonial troops were used in frontline combat alongside Italian regular forces and provided valuable support in the challenging terrain of North Africa.

The Italo-Turkish War was a relatively short but significant conflict that involved the use of various new weapons and tactics. The use of aircraft, naval warfare, mobile warfare, siege warfare, and colonial troops were notable features of the conflict and influenced the outcome of the war, resulting in Italy gaining control over the territories of Tripolitania, Cyrenaica, and the Dodecanese islands.

Mexican-American War (1846 – 1848)

The Mexican-American War was a conflict between the United States and Mexico that took place from 1846 to 1848. It resulted in the United States gaining significant territories, including present-day California, Texas, New Mexico, Arizona, Nevada, Utah, and parts of Colorado, Wyoming, Kansas, and Oklahoma.

During the Mexican-American War, both the United States and Mexico utilized various weapons and tactics, some of which were new or innovative for the time. These include:

1. Rifled Muskets: Both sides made use of rifled muskets in limited quantities, which were an advancement over smoothbore muskets. Due to the greater industrial capacity the United States had somewhat more.

2. Artillery: Both the United States and Mexico used artillery in the form of cannons and howitzers during the war. Artillery played a significant role in battles and sieges, with both sides employing

various types of cannons and howitzers for bombardment, siege warfare, and field battles.

3. Guerrilla Warfare: The Mexican forces made extensive use of guerrilla warfare tactics, including hit-and-run attacks, ambushes, and raids. Mexican irregular forces, known as guerrillas or guerilleros, often targeted American supply lines, communications, and isolated units. This unconventional form of warfare posed challenges for the American forces, who had to adapt their tactics to counter guerrilla tactics.

4. Amphibious Operations: The United States employed amphibious operations, utilizing naval forces to transport troops and conduct landings along the Mexican coast. This included the famous siege of Veracruz, where American forces conducted a successful amphibious assault to capture the city.

5. Mobile Warfare: Both the United States and Mexico utilized mobile warfare tactics, including cavalry and infantry, to conduct maneuver warfare and gain advantages on the battlefield. Mobile warfare allowed for rapid movement, flanking maneuvers, and raids, influencing the outcome of battles and campaigns.

6. Naval Blockade: The United States implemented a naval blockade of Mexican ports to disrupt Mexican trade and communications. The blockade limited Mexico's ability to import supplies and

receive reinforcements, putting additional pressure on Mexican forces.

The Mexican-American War saw the use of various new weapons and tactics that influenced the conduct and outcome of the conflict. The utilization of rifled muskets, artillery, guerrilla warfare, amphibious operations, mobile warfare, and naval blockade were notable features of the war, shaping the strategies and tactics employed by both sides.

Mexican Revolution (1910 – 1920)

The Mexican Revolution was a major armed struggle that took place in Mexico from 1910 to 1920, resulting in significant political, social, and economic changes in the country. The conflict involved various factions and groups with different ideologies, motivations, and goals, including rebel groups, revolutionary leaders, and government forces. Here are some key features and characteristics of the Mexican Revolution, including new weapons and tactics used during the conflict:

Weapons:

1. Automatic Firearms: The Mexican Revolution saw the use of automatic firearms, such as the newly invented machine guns, which had a significant impact on the nature of warfare during the conflict. Machine guns, such as the Maxim and Colt-Browning, were used by both government forces and revolutionary groups, providing increased firepower and changing the dynamics of battles.

2. Modern Rifles: During the Mexican Revolution, modern rifles were used by various factions, including the Winchester Model 1894 and the Mauser Model 1895, which were more accurate and had longer effective ranges compared to older firearms. These rifles were utilized by both government forces and revolutionary groups, improving their firepower and combat capabilities.

3. Artillery: Artillery, such as cannons and mortars, were also employed during the Mexican Revolution, providing significant firepower and strategic advantages to the forces that possessed them. Artillery was used in both offensive and defensive operations, and had a significant impact on the outcome of battles and engagements.

4. Railroads: Both government forces and revolutionary groups utilized railroads to rapidly move troops to various regions of the country and respond to changing battlefronts. Rail transport enabled faster and more efficient movement of troops and supplies, allowing for strategic mobility and flexibility in military operations.

Tactics:

1. Guerrilla Warfare: The Mexican Revolution saw the extensive use of guerrilla warfare tactics by various revolutionary groups. Guerrilla warfare involved hit-and-run attacks, ambushes, and other unconventional tactics that aimed to harass, weaken, and demoralize enemy forces.

Revolutionary leaders, such as Emiliano Zapata and Pancho Villa, utilized guerrilla tactics to great effect against the more conventional forces of the Mexican government.

2. Mass Mobilization: The Mexican Revolution witnessed the mass mobilization of different segments of society, including peasants, workers, indigenous groups, and other marginalized populations. This widespread mobilization of people from diverse backgrounds and regions resulted in large-scale uprisings, protests, and armed movements against the government and other established powers.

3. Political Propaganda: Propaganda played a significant role in the Mexican Revolution, with revolutionary leaders and groups using various media, such as newspapers, posters, and speeches, to spread their ideologies, motivations, and goals. Political propaganda was used to galvanize support, garner sympathy, and mobilize people to join the revolutionary cause.

4. Foreign Support: Some revolutionary groups sought and received support from foreign powers during the Mexican Revolution. For example, Pancho Villa received support from the United States, while Emiliano Zapata received support from foreign anarchists and socialists. This external support influenced the tactics and strategies of the revolutionary groups, and had an impact on the outcome of the conflict.

In summary, the Mexican Revolution was a complex armed struggle that involved various factions and groups, and witnessed the use of new weapons and tactics. Automatic firearms, modern rifles, artillery, guerrilla warfare, mass mobilization, political propaganda, and foreign support were among the key features and characteristics of the conflict. The Mexican Revolution resulted in significant political, social, and economic changes in Mexico, shaping the country's history for years to come.

Opium Wars (1839 – 1842, 1856 – 1860)

The Opium Wars were a series of conflicts that occurred in the mid-19th century between China and Western powers, primarily Britain, over issues related to trade, opium, and diplomatic relations. Here is a brief description of the Opium Wars and some of the new weapons or tactics used by the parties involved.

First Opium War (1839-1842)

Background: The conflict was triggered by the Chinese government's efforts to suppress the illegal opium trade that was causing widespread addiction among the Chinese population. British merchants were heavily involved in the opium trade, and when their opium stocks were confiscated by Chinese authorities, it led to a military confrontation.

New Weapons/Tactics:

- Steamships: The British employed steam-powered warships, including gunboats and steam frigates, which gave them a significant advantage in terms of mobility and firepower. Steamships allowed for faster movement and more effective blockade of Chinese ports.

- **Technologically Advanced Naval Artillery:** The British had superior naval artillery, including rifled guns and explosive shells, which gave them an edge in naval engagements. These advanced artillery pieces had longer range, greater accuracy, and higher lethality compared to the Chinese artillery.

- **Congreve Rockets:** The British also used Congreve rockets, a type of early rocket artillery, in naval and land-based attacks. These rockets were capable of delivering incendiary and explosive payloads, causing significant damage to Chinese fortifications and naval vessels.

- **Naval Blockade:** The British implemented a naval blockade of key Chinese ports, cutting off maritime trade routes and disrupting Chinese economy and supplies. This tactic put pressure on the Chinese government and weakened their ability to resist.

Second Opium War (1856-1860)

Background: The Second Opium War was sparked by a series of incidents involving foreign diplomatic envoys in China. It involved a broader coalition of Western powers, including Britain, France, and the United States, against China.

New Weapons/Tactics:

- Modern Firearms: Western forces were armed with advanced firearms, including rifled muskets, breech-loading rifles, and revolvers. These modern firearms had greater accuracy, range, and firepower compared to the outdated muskets and matchlocks used by the Chinese forces.

- Improved Artillery: Western forces had access to more advanced artillery, including rifled field guns and howitzers, which were more effective in siege warfare and field battles compared to the Chinese artillery.

- Combined Arms Operations: Western forces employed combined arms operations, including coordinated infantry, artillery, and naval attacks, which allowed for greater tactical flexibility and effectiveness on the battlefield.

- Expeditionary Warfare: Western powers conducted expeditionary warfare, projecting force far from their home bases to attack Chinese coastal fortifications and key cities. This allowed them to strike deep into Chinese territory and weaken the Chinese resistance.

- Guerrilla Warfare: Chinese forces used guerrilla warfare tactics, including ambushes, hit-and-run attacks, and harassment of enemy supply lines. This was a more decentralized and flexible approach to warfare compared to traditional Chinese military doctrine, but it was not enough to counter the advanced weaponry and tactics used by the Western forces.

In summary, the Opium Wars saw the use of various new weapons and tactics by the Western powers involved, including steamships, modern firearms, improved artillery, naval blockade, combined arms operations, and expeditionary warfare. The Chinese forces, on the other hand, relied on more traditional military methods, including fortifications, muskets, and guerrilla warfare, but were ultimately outmatched by the superior technology and tactics of the Western forces.

Russo-Japanese War (1904 – 1905)

The Russo-Japanese War was a conflict that took place between the Russian Empire and the Empire of Japan from 1904 to 1905. It was the first major war of the 20th century and marked a significant shift in warfare, with the use of new weapons and tactics. Here is a brief description of the Russo-Japanese War and some of the new weapons or tactics used by the parties involved.

Background: The Russo-Japanese War was primarily fought over rival imperialistic ambitions in Manchuria and Korea, as well as access to strategic ports in the Pacific Ocean.

New Weapons/Tactics:

1. Modern Firearms: Both the Russian and Japanese forces were armed with modern firearms, including bolt-action rifles and machine guns. These weapons had greater accuracy, range, and

firepower compared to the older muzzle-loading rifles and smoothbore muskets used in previous conflicts. The use of modern firearms significantly increased the lethality and effectiveness of infantry units in battle.

2. Naval Warfare: The Russo-Japanese War saw the use of modern naval warfare, with both sides employing advanced warships, including armored cruisers, battleships, and torpedo boats. The use of steam-powered ships, advanced artillery, and torpedoes greatly impacted naval battles and strategies during the war.

3. Siege Warfare: The Russo-Japanese War witnessed the use of modern siege warfare techniques, including trench warfare, entrenchments, and fortifications. Both sides utilized these tactics to defend and assault fortified positions, leading to prolonged battles and high casualties.

4. Cavalry: Cavalry still played a role in the Russo-Japanese War, but it was less prominent compared to earlier conflicts. The advent of modern firearms and machine guns made cavalry charges less effective and more vulnerable to enemy fire. However, cavalry units were still used for reconnaissance, mobility, and harassment of enemy supply lines.

5. Guerrilla Warfare: Japanese forces employed guerrilla warfare tactics, including hit-and-run attacks, ambushes, and raids on enemy supply

lines. These tactics allowed the Japanese to disrupt Russian lines of communication and supply, and inflict significant damage on the Russian forces.

6. Naval Blockade: The Japanese navy effectively blockaded the Russian Pacific Fleet at Port Arthur, cutting off their supplies and reinforcements, and isolating them from the main Russian forces. The naval blockade was a key tactic used by the Japanese to weaken and ultimately defeat the Russian fleet.

7. Medical Evacuation: The Russo-Japanese War saw the introduction of modern medical evacuation techniques, including field hospitals, ambulance trains, and improved medical care for wounded soldiers. This helped to reduce mortality rates among wounded soldiers and improve overall medical care during the conflict.

In conclusion, the Russo-Japanese War saw the use of new weapons and tactics, including modern firearms, naval warfare, siege warfare, cavalry, guerrilla warfare, naval blockade, and medical evacuation. These innovations in warfare had a significant impact on the conduct and outcome of the conflict, and marked a transition towards more modern and sophisticated methods of warfare in the early 20th century.

Russo-Turkish War (1877-1878)

The Russo-Turkish War of 1877 was fought between the Russian Empire and the Ottoman Empire in the Balkans. The primary cause of the war was the Ottoman Empire's inability to implement reforms and maintain control over the various ethnic groups within its borders. The war ended with the Treaty of San Stefano, which significantly reduced the Ottoman Empire's territory and granted independence to several Balkan states: Serbia, Montenegro, Romania, Bulgaria, and Bosnia and Herzegovina other territories under Austro-Hungarian administration.

Both sides used a variety of new weapons and tactics during the conflict. The Russian Empire deployed modern artillery, including the M1867 Krupp breechloading rifled cannon which proved effective in breaking through Ottoman lines, and the Russian Model 1870 Berdan Rifle. The Russians also used telegraphs to communicate and coordinate their movements on the battlefield.

The Ottoman Empire relied heavily on the Chassepot rifle, which had been adopted by the French army in 1866. The Chassepot had a longer range and more accurate fire than the Russian Model 1870 Berdan Rifle. However, the Ottoman forces lacked adequate supplies of ammunition and had difficulty keeping up with the rapid pace of modern warfare.

Overall, the Russo-Turkish War of 1877 marked a turning point in European military history, as both sides demonstrated the effectiveness of new weapons and tactics, including modern artillery and telegraph communication, in achieving military success.

Serbo-Bulgarian War (1885 – 1886)

The Serbo-Bulgarian War was a brief armed conflict that took place between the Kingdom of Serbia and the Kingdom of Bulgaria in 1885.

Background: The Serbo-Bulgarian War was primarily fought over the disputed territory of Eastern Rumelia, which had been a province under the Ottoman Empire but had recently declared its independence. Bulgaria and Serbia both sought to annex Eastern Rumelia, which led to tensions and ultimately resulted in armed conflict.

New Weapons:

- The Serbo-Bulgarian War saw the use of various new weapons and technologies for that time period, although there were no significant breakthroughs in military technology during the conflict.

- Both sides primarily used infantry weapons such as rifles, artillery, and cavalry for combat.

- The repeating rifles, such as the Serbian M1870 Peabody-Martini and the Bulgarian M1870 Berdan, were considered relatively modern weapons during that time period and provided advantages in terms of firepower and rate of fire compared to older single-shot rifles.

Tactics:

- The Serbo-Bulgarian War saw the use of traditional military tactics for that time period, with both sides relying on infantry, cavalry, and artillery for combat.

- One notable tactical development during the war was the use of flanking maneuvers and attempts to outmaneuver the enemy to gain positional advantage.

- The war also saw the use of fortifications and trenches, although they were not extensively used as in later conflicts such as World War I.

Outcome: The Serbo-Bulgarian War ended with a Bulgarian victory, as they successfully annexed Eastern Rumelia. However, the war had broader implications for the balance of power in the Balkans, as it heightened tensions among various regional powers and contributed to the complex political dynamics leading up to the Balkan Wars and eventually World War I.

Overall, the Serbo-Bulgarian War was a relatively short conflict with no major innovations in military technology or tactics. However, it played a role in shaping the political landscape of the Balkans in the late 19th century and set the stage for further conflicts in the region.

Spanish-American War (1898)

The Spanish-American War was a conflict that took place in 1898 between Spain and the United States. It resulted in the defeat of Spain and the cession of several territories, including the Philippines, Guam, and Puerto Rico, to the United States.

New Weapons:

1. Gatling Gun: The Gatling gun, which was an early type of machine gun, was used by the United States during the Spanish-American War. It was capable of firing multiple rounds per minute and provided a significant advantage in terms of firepower compared to traditional firearms.

2. Smokeless Powder: The Spanish-American War was one of the first conflicts where smokeless powder was widely used. Smokeless powder, which replaced the older black powder, produced less smoke when fired, which reduced the visibility of troops on the battlefield and made it harder for the enemy to locate and target them.

3. New Naval Armaments: The Spanish-American War saw the use of modern naval armaments, including steel warships, torpedoes, and mines. The U.S. Navy, in particular, had modern naval vessels equipped with the latest technology, such as the newly developed steel-hulled warships and advanced naval guns.

Tactics:

1. Naval Blockade: The United States used a naval blockade to effectively cut off Cuba, which was a Spanish colony at the time, from receiving reinforcements or supplies from Spain. This strategy limited the ability of Spanish forces in Cuba to receive support and resupply, and ultimately contributed to the U.S. victory in the war.

2. Amphibious Assaults: The U.S. military used amphibious assaults to land troops and supplies on the coast of Cuba and the Philippines. This involved coordinated landings from sea to land, utilizing naval vessels to transport troops and equipment and establish beachheads for further operations. Amphibious assaults allowed the U.S. forces to gain a strategic advantage in terms of mobility and flexibility in conducting military operations.

3. Guerrilla Warfare: In Cuba and the Philippines local forces used guerrilla warfare tactics against the superior Spanish forces, including hit-and-run attacks, ambushes, and sabotage. These tactics allowed them to compensate for their inferior weaponry and military capabilities and put up a formidable resistance against the Spanish forces.

In conclusion, the Spanish-American War saw the use of new weapons such as the Gatling gun and smokeless powder, as well as modern naval armaments. Tactics such as naval blockade, amphibious assaults, and guerrilla warfare were also employed during the conflict, shaping the outcome of the war and influencing future military strategies and technologies.

Texas War of Independence (1835 – 1836)

The Texas War of Independence, also known as the Texas Revolution, was fought between Mexico and the rebellious Mexican province of Texas. In 1835 the Texian rebels fought and won a number of small engagements with local Mexican forces, and in December defeated the Mexican garrison at San Antonio, then the capital of the province.

Santa Anna, who had successfully defeated similar rebellions in other parts of Mexico, decided to deal harshly with the Texians perhaps in order to make an example of them to deter further rebellions. In February of 1836, Santa Anna entered the rebellious province with an army of around 6,000 men catching the Texians unprepared. Santa Anna sent General José de Urrea to the coastal region to cut-off rebels there, and Santa Anna himself led the rest of the force to San Antonio and besieged and defeated the small Texian garrison at the Alamo. During February and March of 1836 the Texians suffered disastrous defeats and the Mexican forces executed many captured rebels including those defending the Alamo and those at Goliad.

In March of 1836 Texas declared independence, and appointed Sam Houston to be the General of its army.

Sam Houston avoided the Mexican army while training his troops. In April of 1836, after leading the Mexican

army on an exhausting chase across Texas, Sam
Houston launched a surprise attack upon the weary
Mexican army encamped in a very poor location at San
Jacinto, close to modern day Houston, Texas. The
Mexican army was defeated, many of the Mexican
soldiers were killed, and Santa Anna himself taken
prisoner and forced to sign a peace treaty accepting the
independence of the Republic of Texas.

When Santa Anna was released and returned to Mexico,
he rejected the treaty he had signed and refused to
accept the independence of Texas. Although the Battle
of San Jacinto is considered to be the end of the War of
Texas Independence, fighting continued for many years
afterwards.

The Battle of San Jacinto Scenario:

Mexicans are surprised and Texians can advance to within 200 meters before the Mexicans respond.

a. Texian Rebels at the Battle of San Jacinto	Points
1 Brilliant General x 6.0 (Sam Houston)	6.0
8 Average Infantry x 2.5	20.0
2 Average Infantry w/rifle (+100m) x 3.0	6.0
1 Average Cavalry x 3.0	3.0
1 Basic Artillery x 3.0	3.0
Total:	38.0

b. Mexican Army at the Battle of San Jacinto	Points
1 Poor General x 2.0 (Santa Anna)	2.0
1 Average Sub-General x 2.0 (Martin de Cos)	2.0
8 Average Infantry x 2.5	20.0
4 Inferior Regular Infantry x 2.0	8.0
2 Average Cavalry x 3.0	6.0
2 Basic Artillery x 3.0	6.0
Total:	44.0

War of the Triple Alliance (1864 – 1870)

The War of the Triple Alliance set Paraguay against Argentina, Brazil and Uruguay. It was an incredibly lopsided contest with Paraguay having a population of less than 500,000 against Brazil with over 9 million, Argentina with 2 million, and Uruguay with 250,000.

The conflict started out with Paraguay having what seemed to be an economic and military advantage against its neighbors. Some referred to Paraguay as the Prussia of South America due its large military and financial advantage in comparison to its neighbors. This initial dominance gave the Paraguayans a confidence that lead not only to very aggressive military actions against its neighbors, but in hindsight suicidal behavior.

Sadly, the Paraguayan reputation for military supremacy was based more upon past successes. Under the President, Solano Lopez, the Paraguayan military had been allowed to degrade for political reasons. Although Paraguay's army was large compared to those of its neighbors, its forces were poorly trained, many units were undermanned, and its weapons mostly old and outdated.

Paraguay started the war against Brazil during the last few months of 1864 supposedly in defense of its ally Uruguay. Brazil supported a revolution in Uruguay. Paraguay launched an attack north into Mato Grosso state of Brazil, but found it difficult to come to the aid of Uruguay. As the fighting against Brazil turned difficult in Mato Grosso, Uruguay fell to the Brazilian backed rebels before Paraguayan aid could arrive. Then in March of 1865 Paraguay foolishly invaded Argentina which wanted to remain neutral bringing it into the war on the side of the Brazilians and Uruguayans creating the Triple Alliance against Paraguay.

Paraguay was now outnumbered, surrounded, and blockaded by river and sea. Its early aggressiveness turned to defeats that destroyed its initial army with most of its modern weapons. Paraguay was short on supplies and military equipment. To make matters worse, in June of 1865 Paraguay suffered a naval defeat to the Brazilians losing most of its best warships.

The war continued and Paraguay suffered more defeats with occasional victories. By 1867 the Paraguayan army had collapsed, and the fighting became more of a guerrilla/resistance war against impossible odds. The President of Paraguay, Solano Lopez, and his 16 year old son were killed in one of the last battles of the war.

The war is marked by stark contrasts between modern and ancient weapons; breech loading artillery, ironclad warships, observation balloons, and breech loading rifles, as compared to barefoot soldiers fighting with machetes and sharpened bamboo spears.

The Paraguayans were not just defeated but almost annihilated. There is considerable debate about Paraguayan losses with some estimates as high as 400,000 casualties (remember it started the war with less than 500,000 people).

It is difficult to come up with helpful army lists:

Paraguay: At the beginning of the war things are a bit clearer. The Paraguayan army numbered perhaps 30,000 poorly armed men with old style muzzle loading muskets (perhaps many flintlocks) with one regiment of about 250 men armed with advanced breech loading rifles. There is a considerable amount of artillery, perhaps 400 mostly old outdated smooth bore muzzle loading pieces. After the first year of fighting the Paraguayan army weapons got worse with many being armed with nothing more than machetes and sharpened bamboo spears.

The Alliance forces: When the war began there was a disorganized Brazilian standing army of perhaps 16,000 men (but a large national guard), an Argentine standing army of about 8,500 men, and a Uruguayan standing army of less than 2,000 men. By then end of the war the Brazilian army numbered almost 150,000. The numbers for Argentina and Uruguay are not clear.

All sides suffered horrendous losses due to disease more than to battle, even though Paraguay lost more as a percentage of its population (some numbers go as high as 90%???).

Milton Keynes UK
Ingram Content Group UK Ltd.
UKHW040632280723
425958UK00001B/105